CAN YOU

think of a four-let[ter ...]
in ENY?

find an anagram for TARELBA[...]

(see solution No. 10)

IS IT POSSIBLE TO

send messages faster than the speed of light?

live after your heart has stopped beating?

make water flow uphill?

ride a bicycle upside down?

live through the same day twice?

sail faster than the wind?

(see solution No. 70)

CAN YOU

find the fifth term in the following series?
77, 49, 36, 18, . . .

(see solution No. 77)

Fawcett Gold Medal Books
by L. H. Longley-Cook

FUN FOR PUZZLE PEOPLE
FUN WITH BRAIN PUZZLERS
WORK THIS ONE OUT

Fun with
Brain
Puzzlers

by L. H. Longley-Cook

A FAWCETT GOLD MEDAL BOOK
Fawcett Publications, Inc., Greenwich, Conn.

Contents

v

PUZZLERS

1: Don't Spend It All At Once

If I start with $10 and spend all but $3, how much do I have left?

2: Nine Boxes

In Figure 1 a line has been drawn through the center of each of nine equally spaced boxes using five straight lines which have been drawn without lifting the pencil from the paper. Can you do this with only four straight lines under the same condition of not lifting the pencil from the paper?

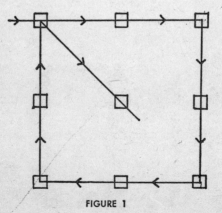

FIGURE 1

3: At the Five and Ten

I bought some items at the Five and Ten. All the items were the same price and I bought as many items as the number of cents in the cost of each item. My bill was $2.25. How many items did I buy?

4: A Match Problem

In the arrangement of matches shown in Figure 2, there are four small squares and one large square, making five squares in all. Can you reposition three matches to reduce the number to three?

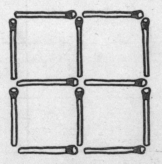

FIGURE 2

5: Hands of a Clock

How many times do the two hands of a clock point in the same direction between 6:00 A.M. and 6:00 P.M. of a single day?

6: Counting Squares

Can you count how many complete squares there are in Figure 3? At first it is tempting to say there are sixteen in the main plan, plus two superimposed squares, making eighteen in all. Then with some thought you will see eight more. What is the full total?

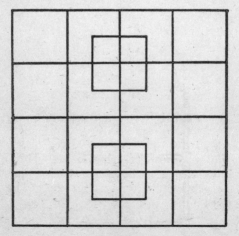

FIGURE 3

7: Letters for Digits

In the following subtraction problem each digit has been replaced by a certain letter. Can you reconstruct the original problem?

$$
\begin{array}{r}
A B A \\
- C A \\
\hline
A B
\end{array}
$$

8: Which Games Do They Play?

Of three friends two play golf, two bowl and two play tennis. The one who does not play tennis does not bowl and the one who does not bowl does not play golf. Which games does each friend play?

9: My Checking Account

My bank has been charging me 25 cents a month plus 10 cents a check for my checking account. The bank now tells me it will charge, in the future, 50 cents a month plus 8 cents a check and this will save me money. How many checks must I draw a month for this to be true?

10: Four Word Problems

(1) Can you think of a four-letter word ending in ENY?

(2) Can you think of a word with three pairs of letters in a row?

(3) Can you arrange three of one letter and three of another letter to make a six-letter word?

(4) Can you find an anagram for TARELBAY?

11: How Old Is My Daughter?

My daughter is twice as old as my son and half as old as I am. In twenty-two years my son will be half my age. How old is my daughter?

12: Dice

A die lying on a table looks like that in Figure 4. What number is on the side face down on the table?

FIGURE 4

13: Another Match Problem

Can you move just one match in Figure 5 and make the
relationship approximately correct?

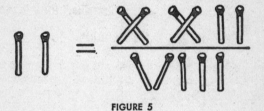

FIGURE 5

14: Some Series

Find the rule for each of these series and write down
what the next term will be.

(1)	8	11	14	17	20	23
(2)	6	9	18	21	42	45
(3)	12	9	3	6	3	1

15: Can You?

"We eat what we can, and we can what we can't."
Can you explain who could make this statement?

16: The Striking Clock

I woke up one night and heard my clock strike "one." I was too lazy to turn on the light to see what time it was. As I lay there pondering, it occurred to me to speculate how long I would have to lie awake in order to be sure what was the exact time. My clock strikes the hours and strikes "one" each half hour. I fell asleep before I solved the problem, but can you work out what is the longest time I would have to lie awake after hearing the strike "one," to be sure of the time?

17: Ages

Bill and his brother Jim have combined ages of 30. In fourteen years Jim will be three times the age Bill is now. How old is Jim?

18: Relations

(1) Is it legal for a man to marry his widow's sister?

(2) Brothers and sisters have I none, but this man is my father's son. Who is "this man"?

(3) "Jean is my niece," said Jack to his sister Jill. "She is not my niece," said Jill. Can you explain?

19: Paper Cutting

Starting with a square piece of paper, I trim the corners and throw my trimmings away so as to leave the largest possible circular piece of paper. Starting again with this circular piece of paper, I again trim it and throw the pieces away so as to leave the largest possible square piece of paper which can be cut from the circle. How much of the original square piece of paper is cut off and thrown away?

20: Skiing

Going up on the ski lift, I travel at 5 miles an hour; coming down the ski slope I travel at an average speed of 25 miles an hour. If the ski slope is the same length as the ski lift, and I ignore any time I waste at the top, what is my average speed for the round trip?

21: School Notes

If 6 boys fill 6 notebooks in 6 weeks and 4 girls fill 4 notebooks in 4 weeks, how many notebooks will a class of 12 boys and 12 girls fill in 12 weeks?

22: A Different Type of Maze

In Figure 6, there are two points labeled "A," two labeled "B," two labeled "C," two labeled "D," and two labeled "E." Can you join A to A, B to B, C to C, etc., by following lines on the grid so that no two routes intersect, cross or touch?

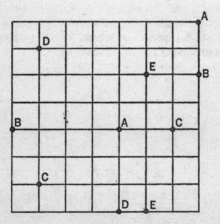

FIGURE 6

23: Three Friends

Three friends, Thomas, Richard and John are different ages. Thomas is a bachelor. Richard earns less than the youngest of the three. The oldest of the three earns most but has the cost of putting his son through college.

Who is the oldest and who is the youngest of the three friends?

24: A Teen-age Club

Members of a local teen-age club disagreed about the way a certain outing was managed and 15 girls withdrew. This left two boys for each girl. The boys were unhappy about the new setup and 45 moved out, leaving only one boy for each five girls. I fear the club will soon disband. Can you work out how many girls there were in the club at the time of the outing?

25: The Two Wrestlers

Red-haired Lord John Brougham, the famous wrestler whose real name is John Smith, entered the Two Gun Bar with his old friend, golden-haired Battling Thompson, whose real name is Jones. Thompson's son's father is Lord John. How can this be explained?

26: Simple Geometry

In Figure 7, O is the center of the circle and AB is parallel to OD. AO and BC are perpendicular to OD. OC is 5 units long and CD is 1 unit long. Find the length of AC.

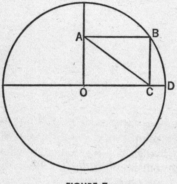

FIGURE 7

27: Tom, Dick and Harry

Tom, Dick and Harry are three friends. Their last names are Smith, Jones, and Robinson, but not necessarily respectively. They all go shopping one Saturday and Tom spends exactly twice as much as Dick and Dick spends exactly twice as much as Harry. Smith spends exactly $12.65 more than Robinson. What is each man's full name?

28: Going to Town

One day last week I went to town. I had my hair cut, bought one of the local weekly papers, which had been published that day, bought some grapes at the Farmer's Market and some miscellaneous things at the drugstore. I cashed a check for $50 at the bank.

The barber is closed on Mondays, the bank is closed on Saturdays and Sundays. The Farmer's Market is open on Mondays, Wednesdays and Saturdays. The drugstore is closed only on Sundays. On which day of the week did I go to town?

29: No Change

Looking at the coins in my pocket, I noticed that I could pay the exact price for any item from one cent up to and including one dollar without receiving any change. What is the fewest number of coins I could have had in my pocket?

30: My Four Children

Bill, my second oldest, is twice as old as one of my three other children, expressing their ages, as is customary, in complete number of years.

Joan is three times as old as one of the other two children, John and Jean.

John is four times as old as Jean, who is 1 year old. How old is Bill?

31: Crossing the Line

In Figure 8 there is no difficulty in drawing a continuous line which crosses each line segment (e.g., AB, BC, CF, etc.) once and only once. But it is impossible to draw a similar line in Figure 9. For example, the line drawn fails to cross the segment EF. Can you draw a line crossing each line segment in Figure 10?

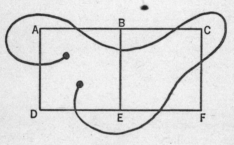

FIGURE 8

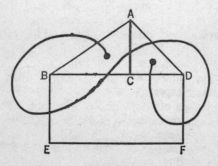

FIGURE 9

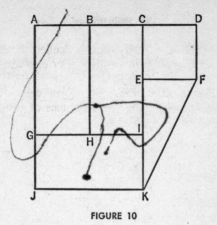

FIGURE 10

32: The Collectors

Mr. Brown, Mr. Smith and Mr. Jones are banker, lawyer and doctor, but not necessarily respectively.

The Browns and the Smiths play bridge each Friday night.

The Smiths know the Joneses well.

The banker collects stamps; the lawyer old silver; and the doctor early American prints.

The lawyer and the doctor have never met.

Mr. Jones has never heard of a hallmark.

What is the profession of each man?

33: Palindromes

A palindrome is a word which is spelled the same way whether read backward or forward. For example,

$$NOON$$

is a palindrome. Can you write down eight four-letter palindromes without using proper names or slang words?

34: Simple Algebra

Given $x = 1$ and $y = 1$, we have
$$x = y$$
Multiplying each side by x
$$x^2 = xy$$
Subtracting y^2 from each side
$$x^2 - y^2 = xy - y^2$$
Factorizing each side
$$(x + y)(x - y) = y(x - y)$$
Dividing out the common term $(x - y)$ we have
$$x + y = y$$
Substituting the given values
$$1 + 1 = 1$$
$$\text{or} \quad 2 = 1$$
What is wrong with this proof?

35: Letter Addition

In the following addition each digit has been replaced by a letter. Can you determine which digit each letter represents and reconstruct the problem?

$$
\begin{array}{r}
A B C \\
A B \\
A A \\
\hline
D E E A
\end{array}
$$

36: The Round Window

A designer is planning a nine-paned round window for a church on the plan in Figure 11. He decides that the window would be aesthetically correct if the area of each of the eight outer panes was equal to the area of the circular inner pane. Assuming the inner circular pane is 2 feet in diameter and the thickness of the wood between the panes can be ignored, what should be the length in inches of the spokes which separate the outer panes?

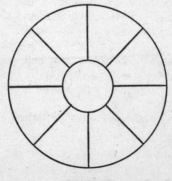

FIGURE 11

37: Fencing the Yard

Mr. Brown's suburban home is on a corner where two streets meet. He has a 200-foot frontage onto each street. His driveway, which is 8 feet wide, is exactly in the middle of one of these frontages. Mr. Brown decides to place a post and rail fence along these two sides of his property, leaving only a gap for the driveway, so that his children will not run carelessly into the street. The fence Mr. Brown chooses has three rails in each section. The rails are 9 feet long and go through precut slots in the posts so that the overall length of a section is 8 feet from center of post to center of post.

How many rails and how many posts must Mr. Brown buy?

38: The Newlyweds

Our friends, John, Bill, Dick, Carolyn, Maryann and Joan paired off and were married last summer. They are all keen on sports. John was captain of the school football team, Bill is a star basketball player, and Dick is a keen swimmer. Rather surprisingly, however, Dick's wife cannot swim.

Carolyn, who has a good eye for a ball, plays golf as her chief sport. Maryann, who by the way is Dick's sister, is a good dancer and Joan, whose husband is very short, is an expert diver.

Can you work out who is married to whom?

39: Four Triangles

With six sticks of equal length, how can you form four equal-sided triangles without breaking or cutting the sticks?

40: Keeping Account

I was trying to teach my young son to keep a record of his spending, and had explained that he must write down each purchase and the amount of money he had left. As he wanted to buy some things in the 5 and 10, I gave him half a dollar and told him that if he kept his accounts properly in the little notebook I had given him, I would give him an extra 25 cents on his return.

He returned with the following "account" and explained tearfully that he had lost a cent somewhere as he had no money left.

		Money Left
Received	50 cents	
Drawing Book	25 cents	25 cents
Candy	12 cents	13 cents
Pencil	5 cents	8 cents
Eraser	5 cents	3 cents
Crayon	3 cents	. . . .
		——
		49 cents

Where did he lose the cent?

41: Children's Party

Our youngest boy had just come back from a children's party and he was too excited to answer my questions very coherently.

He did recall there were five girls at the party and that Betty had worn blue and Ethel red. He could not remember the color Marge wore but he was sure it was not yellow. He told me that Sheila and the girl in green won a three-legged race against Betty and the girl in yellow. He also said he liked the girl in brown best.

What color did Jane wear and what was the name of the girl our child liked best?

42: Change for a Dollar

A cashier found that she was often asked to give change for a dollar to people who had made no purchases but wanted a dime or two nickels for a telephone call. She started thinking one day about the number of ways she could make change. Business was slack and she turned her thoughts into a definite problem. If she gave no more than four of any coin, in how many different ways could she give change?

43: Earning a Living

A young man (A) is offered a job at a bank at a starting salary of $5,200 per annum (payable weekly). He is told that if his work is satisfactory his salary will be increased by $520 per annum at the end of each year for the next five years. His friend (B) is offered a job at another bank at a starting salary of $2,600 per half year (payable weekly). He is told that if his work is satisfactory, his half-yearly salary will be increased by $130 per half year each half year for the next five years. Is A or B offered the better contract?

44: Can You Thread the Maze?

FIGURE 12

45: Four Men

Mr. Allen, Mr. Baker, Mr. Campbell and Mr. Davis live in Boston, Chicago, San Francisco, and Washington, but not necessarily respectively.

Mr. Davis lives closer to Mr. Allen than he does to Mr. Campbell or Mr. Baker.

Mr. Allen is a travel agent; Mr. Baker is a cable car driver; Mr. Campbell is an F.B.I. agent; and Mr. Davis works on an embassy staff.

In what city does each man live?

46: Do You Know?

(1) When you travel from the Atlantic Ocean to the Pacific Ocean through the Panama Canal, do you go from east to west or from west to east?

(2) When you look to Windsor, Canada, across the Detroit River from the city of Detroit, do you look north, south, east or west?

(3) Which are the most northerly, the most easterly, the most southerly and the most westerly states in the United States?

47: Professor Cubit's Walk

Professor Cubit was telling me about the time he was a visiting professor at the College of Passall. This was in a very small community and there were only four streets, Market, Elm, Oak and Chestnut: "I can still recall the town plan," said the Professor, "and I will draw it for you (See Figure 13). Market Street was all shops and the other three streets were residential. The little house I lived in was to the south of the college chapel and I used to enjoy walking a different way to chapel each morning. There was

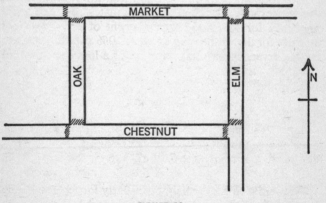

FIGURE 13

very little traffic in Passall, but some officious person had introduced a number of crosswalks for pedestrians, which I
have sketched in on the town plan. One day my walk to the
chapel crossed each crosswalk once and only once. As you
know, I am a very law-abiding person, so I never jaywalk."

On which street did Professor Cubit live, and on which
side of the street was his little house?

48: Selling Appliances

John was being transferred from the East to the West
Coast and decided it was not worth the transportation
cost of taking his old washer and dryer with him. Checking
with advertisements, he determined in his own mind what
their values were. However, the actual prices he received
did not exactly agree with his estimates. He sold each
appliance for $50 and made a profit of 25% over his
estimate for the washer and a loss of 20% over his estimate
for the dryer. Did he make a profit or a loss over his total
estimate?

49: A Dinner Party

We were giving a formal dinner party for ten (including
ourselves) which is a number I always like because the

host can sit at one end of the table and the hostess at the other, and still maintain the correct alternate male and female around the table. My wife was trying to work out the seating. "Tom and Jean have not been here to dinner before so they are the guests of honor. Tom must sit on my right and Jean on your right, but I don't know how I want to seat the others." "Well," I said, "I would like Janet on my left. I have a soft spot for her." "You can have her," replied my wife, "but I will not have her husband Jack next to me; I think he should be next to Maryann."

Since we do not place husbands and wives next to each other, this determined the seating of everyone, including Howard's wife Lois, and Maryann's husband Bill.

Can you work out the seating arrangement?

50: Sunday School Picnic

The local Sunday School picnic is always fun. Male grownups attending are asked to pay 50 cents for refreshments and female grownups 30 cents. The children are charged only 1 cent each. At the last picnic we had a total attendance of 100. Everyone paid the correct charge and total receipts were exactly $10. How many men, women and children attended?

51: Old Friend Hypotenuse

A line is drawn from the corner of a right angle triangle (Figure 14) to the middle of the hypotenuse. Can you prove that its length is one-half the hypotenuse?

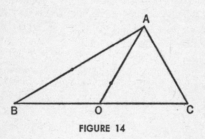

FIGURE 14

52: What Is Wrong?

Why are these statements obviously untrue?

(1) Leander swam the Hellespont seven times each day for exercise.
(2) Astronauts in their flights around the earth are always most tired when they see the sunset.
(3) The first thing the Pilgrim Fathers did when they landed was to plant the Stars and Stripes near Plymouth Rock.
(4) An archaeologist digging in Britain found a Roman coin dated 55 B.C.

53: Dominoes on a Board

A board, 9 inches by 7 inches, is marked out into 63 one-inch squares. To make the number of squares even, the middle square is blocked out by placing a chessman on it. John attempts to cover the board, other than the middle square, with dominoes which are just 2 inches by 1 inch. In Figure 15 he has 11 dominoes in place. Since 31 dominoes will be needed in all, more than one set will be required. Can you completely cover the board, other than the middle square, without having any domino stick out over the edge of the board, or can you prove it cannot be done?

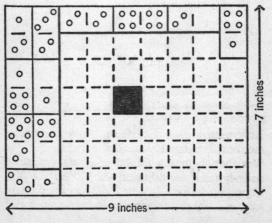

FIGURE 15

54: Winning at Chess

I had promised my young son, Mark, a new bicycle for Christmas but he had been begging me to let him have it earlier. Finally, Mark came to me with the following proposition. "If I can beat you at chess, will you let me have a new bicycle now?" Since Mark had not been playing chess very long and I was quite an expert, I told him not to be silly, since he could not possibly win. He replied, "I do not mean I will beat you every time we play, but I will undertake that if we play two games, I will win at least one or draw both games." Feeling that Mark must be taught that chess was a difficult game and he could not possibly beat me if I tried, I agreed to his proposal.

Mark said he wanted to play the two games simultaneously, each of us making alternate moves on alternate boards. I was to play white on Board A and black on Board B and was to start first. I could see no reason to object to this. How did Mark succeed in winning his bicycle?

55: Do You Know Your Calendar?

(1) How many years were there between January 1, 5 B.C. and January 1, A.D. 5?
(2) Was there a time when 10 or 11 days were skipped entirely from the calendar?
(3) Counting January 1, A.D. 2000 as one, January 2 as two, etc., what number should be assigned to March 1, A.D. 2000?

56: Which Is the Even Way?

In Figure 16, towns are represented by dots and the only roads connecting them are represented by lines. The problem is to find the way from A to B which passes through the fewest number of towns, with the requirement that *an even number of towns must be passed en route.*

For example, the route along the top of the plan is no solution because it passes through 3 towns.

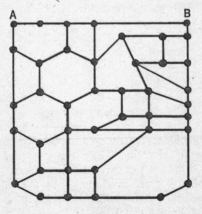

FIGURE 16

57: Suburban Commuting

We have an excellent suburban commuting service except that the rolling stock is very ancient. The stations are close together and the train seems to have hardly reached full speed before it is slowing down for the next station.

Recently it was proposed that the trains should be speeded up during the rush hour by running skip-stop trains, that is, trains which stopped at every alternate station.

One official objected to the plan. He argued, "It is our policy to run our rush hour trains at such intervals that each train leaves the city fully loaded. With a skip-stop system the trains to any individual station will be half as frequent. Now since there will be twice as many passengers getting out at each station, the train will have to stop twice as long at half the number of stations. Hence, there will be no real speedup of the journey. However, the fewer stops will, I agree, have a psychological advantage."

Was the official correct?

58: For Stamp Collectors

I send a number of overseas letters by Air Mail and the postage is 15 cents. Since many of my friends are philatelists I always put three different 5-cent commemorative stamps on each envelope. With five different commemorative stamps to choose between, how many combinations of stamps can I use?

59: The Flagpole

I was admiring the classical symmetry of our state capitol from the Mall which leads directly to the main entrance. I noticed with surprise that the flagpole which stands centrally in front of the main doorway did not appear to line up with the center of the doorway but with its edge. This apparent lack of symmetry worried me for a little but I soon realized I was standing at the edge of the Mall and not in its center. I started to wonder if I could estimate from this how far the flagpole was from the door. I estimated the doorway was 10 feet across, that the center of the Mall opposite me was 600 yards from the flagpole and that I was 40 feet from the center of the Mall. If my estimates of distances are correct, how far is the flagpole from the main doorway?

60: Shingles and Apples

There is an old story of the trader who put into Philadelphia with a boatload of shingles, some of which had been damaged in passage. He was asked by a Quaker merchant what was the price of his shingles. "They are $10 a bundle," he replied, "if you choose the bundles and $5 a bundle if I choose them." The merchant thought for a minute and said, "Captain, I will buy your whole cargo and you can choose the bundles."

Here is a problem which involves the same principle. A man had an apple stall and he sold his larger apples at 3 for a dollar and his smaller apples at 5 for a dollar. When he had just 30 apples of each size left to sell, he asked his son to look after the stall while he had lunch. When he came back from lunch the apples were all gone and the son gave his father $15. The father questioned his son. "You should have received $10 for the large apples and $6 for the 30 small apples, making $16 in all." The son looked surprised. "I am sure I gave you all the money I received and I counted the change most carefully. It was difficult to manage without you here, and, as there was an equal number of each sized apple left, I sold them all at the average price of 4 for $1. Four into 60 goes 15 times so I am sure $15 is correct."

Where did the $1 go?

61: An Easy Cross-Number Problem

Across

  1 The cube of a whole number.

  5 The number of square inches in a square yard.

  6 The number of cubic inches in a cubic foot.

  7 The number of millimeters in a meter.

Down

  1 A number which is unchanged if the digits are reversed.

  2 A prime number.

  3 The number of feet in a mile.

  4 The number of seconds in an hour.

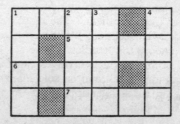

FIGURE 17

62: Our Bank Staff

The manager, the accountant, the teller and the auditor
at our local bank are Mr. Smith, Mr. Brown, Mr. Jones
and Mr. Foster but I can never remember who is who. I do
know that:

Mr. Brown is taller than the auditor or the teller.

The manager lunches alone.

Mr. Jones plays bridge with Mr. Smith.

The tallest of the four plays basketball.

Mr. Foster lunches with the auditor and the teller.

Mr. Smith is older than the auditor.

Mr. Brown plays no sports.

Can you find out which job each man performs?

63: Getting Soft Drinks

I returned home to find 10 boys gathered around the
refrigerator getting soft drinks. As I recognized only my
two children, I asked each boy his name and age. I found
the ages, including those of my children, ranged from 4 to
13 and each boy was a different age. Also I found that
there were two boys from each of 5 families. The sums of
the ages of each pair of brothers were 10, 13, 17, 22, 23.
One of my boys is 7 years old. How old is his brother?

64: Changing Figures

It is interesting to find the rule by which one figure can be changed into another. The following examples illustrate what is meant, where the rule is given for changing A into B.

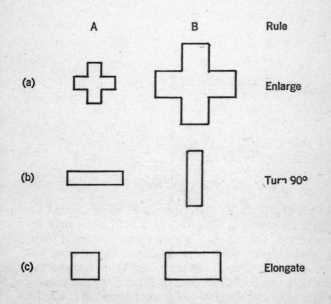

etc.

In the following three examples, find out the rule for changing A into B. Apply the rule to C and determine which of the suggested solutions W, X, Y, and Z is correct.

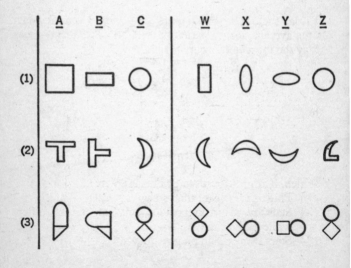

65: Four Readers

Mr. and Mrs. Webster and Mr. and Mrs. Collins each have different tastes in literature. One prefers history, another biography, another detective novels and another adventure stories. Of the four, only two have blue eyes and one of these likes biography best. The wife with blue eyes likes adventure stories and her husband likes history best.

Mr. Collins has brown eyes.

What is Mrs. Collins' taste in literature?

66: Friday the Thirteenth

Friday the thirteenth is reputed to be a very unlucky day. On the average, over a period of years, how frequently does Friday the thirteenth occur?

67: The Planets

Which, if any, of these statements is correct?
(1) Planets are bigger than stars.
(2) Stars are fixed in position relative to each other, while planets move.
(3) Stars twinkle and planets do not.

68: Simple Topology

Topology, sometimes described as the most general of all geometries, is concerned with the connectivity of lines or surfaces. Any two or three dimensional figure which can be changed into another by continuous transformations is the same to the topologist. In terms of topology, the letters A, O, P, Q are the same since they each have one hole in them but differ from B which has two holes and again from E which has none. In three dimensions an anchor ring and a teacup are topologically the same. This very simple little problem may surprise you if you have not seen it before.

Take a loop of string and thread it through the handle of a teacup, as shown in Figure 18, and tie the free ends to some convenient hook. Be sure to use a long piece of string and thread the string through the handle exactly as shown in Figure 18. Can you remove the cup from the string without cutting the string or undoing the knot where the string is tied to the hook?

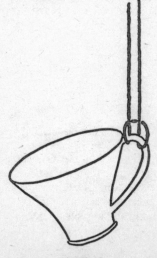

FIGURE 18

69: Star Polygons

Star polygons are always attractive to look at, for example, the regular octagram shown in Figure 19. If we connect, in turn, ADGBEHCFA, the whole figure is drawn without lifting the pencil from the paper. It is not difficult to see that the angle at each point is 45°.

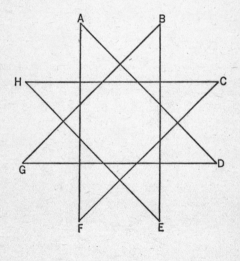

FIGURE 19

While the octagram has eight points, the pentagram shown in Figure 20 has only five points. The star on the Stars and Stripes are regular pentagrams. Can you work out the angle at any one of the five points of a regular pentagram?

FIGURE 20

70: Is It Possible?

Is it possible to:
(1) Send messages faster than the speed of light?
(2) Live after your heart has stopped beating?
(3) Make water flow uphill?
(4) Ride a bicycle upside down?
(5) Live through the same day twice?
(6) Sail faster than wind?

71: Birthday Wishes

My son sent me the following birthday card:

```
H A P P Y
B I R T H
  D A Y
─────────
D T A T H
D A D D Y
─────────
I T X H I
─────────
```

He told me that this was an addition problem with a subtotal, and each letter represented a different digit. Can you find which digit represents which letter?

72: Paying Bills

I received four bills in the mail yesterday. They were from my doctor, my dentist, the drugstore and the hardware store.

The bills from the doctor and the dentist were both an exact amount of dollars and the doctor's bill was half as much again more than the dentist's. I was surprised to note that the dollars in the drugstore bill were exactly the same as the cents in the hardware bill, and the cents in the drugstore bill were exactly the same as the dollars in the hardware bill.

The dentist's bill was the smallest and the drugstore bill the next smallest, and the total of the four bills was $55.25. What was the amount of each bill?

73: Meeting Uncle William

My old uncle William likes to walk over to have lunch with us on Sundays. Recently we felt it was too long a walk for him and I have driven toward his house and picked him up and driven him the last part of the way. Both Uncle William and I are very methodical. He always starts at the same time and walks at the same speed and I start to meet him at the same time and drive at the same speed. As a result, I always pick him up at the same point on the road and get home at the same time. Last Sunday something went wrong. I had to drive farther than usual and returned with him to our house 10 minutes later. When I questioned him, he explained that he had started as usual but had stopped for some time to watch a tree-planting ceremony outside a church he had to pass. If I drive at thirty-six miles an hour and Uncle William walks at three miles an hour, how long did Uncle William spend watching the tree planting?

74: Heads and Tails

Given four coins, what is the probability that exactly two heads will turn up when the coins are all tossed?

75: The Moon

(1)   Walking home from my office one evening, I noticed that I could see just half the face of the moon. How could I tell if this was the first quarter of the moon or the last quarter?

(2)   How often does full moon occur in a year?

(3)   If the distance of the sun from the earth is approximately 93,000,000 miles and its diameter is approximately 860,000 miles, and the distance of the moon from the earth is approximately 240,000 miles, what is the approximate diameter of the moon?

76: Missing Digits

In the following long division problem, X represents any digit from 0 to 9 and . represents a decimal point. Can you reconstruct the division?

```
                    . x x x
        x x x )   x x x .
                  x x x . x
                    . x x x
                    . x x x
```

77: An Unusual Series

Can you find the fifth term in the following series?
$$77, \quad 49, \quad 36, \quad 18, \quad \ldots$$

78: Do You Know Your United States?

(1)   Which is the largest lake wholly within the United States?

(2)   Which is farther west, Pittsburgh or Miami?

(3)   Have any states common borders with eight other states?

(4)   Are any states bounded by four straight borders?

(5)   Is any part of the United States (other than Alaska) north of the 49th parallel?

79: Climbing the Mountain

We were all climbing the local mountain and as we got higher it seemed to get colder and colder.

John said it was due to our greater exposure to the cold winds. Bob said it was something to do with the more rarefied atmosphere. Tom said it was just imagination and as we were nearer the sun it must really be warmer. Bill said we were farther from the center of the earth which was known to be hot. What do you say?

80: Is the Rope Knotted?

A loop of rope is lying on the ground in the position shown in Figure 21. You are too far away to see which section of the rope is above or below at each of the crossovers at A, B and C. If we assume that it is equally likely that either section is on top at each crossover, what is the probability that the rope is knotted?

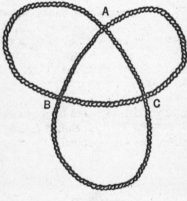

FIGURE 21

81: The Two Rugs

A housewife has two rugs of the same material, one 10 feet by 10 feet and one a long runner 8 feet by 1 foot. How can she make a single continuous cut in the 10 foot by 10 foot rug, so as to form two pieces which, when combined with the 8 foot by 1 foot rug can be stitched into a rug 9 feet by 12 feet? The two rugs are of plain pattern and have a pile on one side only.

82: Lost Deal

Professor Cubit likes to play a card game of his own
invention, not unlike bridge, which involves dealing a pack
of 52 cards clockwise around and around the table into four
piles, starting with the player to the left of the dealer. One
day, when Professor Cubit was dealing, he was called to the
telephone. When he returned he could not recall to which
pile he had last dealt a card. I was about to count each pile
to determine where the next card must fall and one of the
other players suggested we should start the deal over again.
Professor Cubit would have none of this. He said he would
show us how he could complete the deal so that each pile
had thirteen cards without counting the cards in each pile
and without knowing where the deal had stopped when the
telephone rang. Can you think how this could be done?

83: Little League Baseball

In the local little league each member club played each
other member club, and the Devon club, which hopes to
become a member of the league next year, played most of
the clubs in the league. No club played against any club
more than once and in all there were 75 games played.
With how many league clubs was the Devon club unable to
arrange a game?

84: What Shape Is It?

Professor Cubit was telling me about puzzles concerning the shape of a solid body when viewed from various directions. He gave as an example the cube standing on one face which looks like Figure 22, whether viewed from the left or from the front or from above (see Figure 23). He then mentioned that if the cube stood on one of its apexes it

FIGURE 22

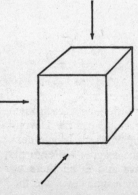

FIGURE 23

would look like Figure 24 from all directions. It is surprising the same body can look so different.

If we take a circular rod 1 inch in diameter and cut a 1-inch length from it, and then shave off the corners so that one end is a straight line like the end of a chisel (see Figure 25), then the silhouette of this body from the left, from the front, and from above will be as shown in Figure 26. However, the view from the front will show the edge of the cut where the corner was shaved off as in Figure 27.

Professor Cubit then posed the following problem. The two drawings in Figure 28 represent an object seen from the left and from the front. Can you suggest what it might look like from above?

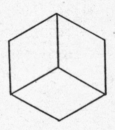

FIGURE 24

FIGURE 25

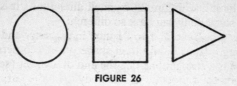

FIGURE 26

FIGURE 27

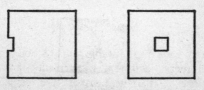

FIGURE 28

85: The Ten Bags

There are ten bags, each containing ten weights, all of which look identical. In nine of the bags each weight is 16 ounces, but in one of the bags the weights are actually 17 ounces each. How is it possible, in a single weighing on an accurate weighing scale, to determine which bag contains the 17-ounce weights?

86: Tom's Class

Tom's class had been questioned on which subjects they liked and disliked, and the results when tabulated were as follows:

                18 liked Mathematics
                32 liked English
                25 liked Languages

Sixteen said they liked both English and Languages but only 7 said they liked both Mathematics and Languages, and only 8 said they like both Mathematics and English. Only 3 said they liked all three subjects and none admitted that he did not like any subject.

How many children are there in Tom's class?

87: Mexican Table Mats

My son gave me a set of table mats he bought in Mexico. They were rectangular and were made of straw circles joined together in the form shown in Figure 29. All the circles on the edges of each mat were white and the inner circles red. I noted that there were 20 white circles and 15 red circles.

I wondered if it were possible to make a mat in this form

where the number of white circles equaled the number of red circles. I found there were two possible solutions. Can you find them and show that there are only two such solutions?

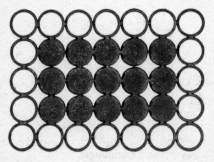

FIGURE 29

88: Russian Roulette

Two gunmen, McGraw and Hipshot, think up the following variation of Russian Roulette. Each will load his sixshooter with from one to five bullets and they will shoot in turn at a target which they cannot miss. Before shooting, each gunman must spin the chambers of his gun so that the odds of any particular chamber being fired are 1/6. The one who hits the target first is the winner and the loser has the task of holding up the local bank.

McGraw is to shoot first. How many bullets should he put in his gun and how many into Hipshot's gun so that each has an equal chance of winning?

89: Hen Laying Problem

Professor Cubit reminds me of the following old riddle:
"If a hen and a half lays an egg and a half in a
day and a half, how many and a half, who lay
better by a half, lay a half-score and a half in a
week and a half?"

90: The Curious Sequence

A friend asks you to continue the following sequence.
                          OTTFFS...
When this suggests nothing to you he adds another term
                          OTTFFSS..
The pairs of letters T T, F F, S S now suggest something,
but you still cannot deduce the sequence. He adds another
term

                     OTTFFSSE.
You are still worried by the initial term O, but otherwise
every other pair of terms seems to run in reverse sequence
through the alphabet (T T, S S, R R, Q Q, ...) and
(F F, E E, D D, C C, ...), so you write down
                 OTTFFSSEERRDD..etc.
What is the real solution?

91: Hex Sign

The hex sign drawn in Figure 30 is made up entirely of
circles 1 inch in radius. Can you calculate the area of each
of the darkly shaded petal-shaped areas?

FIGURE 30

92: Large Numbers

There is no largest number. However large a number may be a larger number can always be obtained by just adding 1 to it. Some very large numbers occur in science. Thus there are approximately

$$602,500,000,000,000,000,000,000$$

molecules in 32 grams (technically 1 mole) of oxygen and we know this result to a greater degree of accuracy than we know the population of any large city. Scientists and mathematicians use a notation to avoid writing large numbers at length. The above number is written 6.025×10^{23}, the 23 signifying that there are 23 digits after the initial digit 6.

Some years ago the astronomer, Professor Edington, postulated that there were $2 \times 136 \times 2^{256}$ particles in the Universe but this postulate is not accepted as having validity.

Large numbers occur also in mathematics. The largest

number the author has discovered which serves a definite purpose, rather than just being a term in some series, is Skewes number which occurs in the theory of prime numbers. This number is

$$10^{10^{10^{34}}}$$

The following is an interesting little puzzle in large numbers. What is the largest number which can be formed by using only four ones, and what is the largest number which can be formed by using only four twos?

93: Professor Cubit's Bets

My friend, Professor Cubit, likes to match quarters and make other small bets with me. In most of these contests I find I win about as often as he does but there are a few of his favorites which seem to offer me fair odds but on which he is more frequently successful than I am. For example:

(1) When we go to get the elevator which takes him from his ivory tower overlooking the campus to lunch, he will press both up and down buttons and bet me that an up car will come first.

(2) Again, when the Professor receives a dollar bill in change he will offer to give me the bill if all eight digits in the serial number are different, if I will pay him a nickel if two or more are the same. With such long odds I feel my chances are good but somehow I keep paying out and very rarely win the dollar.

Can you show why Professor Cubit wins on these two bets?

94: The Bird Cage

There is a well-known story of the person who sees a truck full of live poultry stopped before a bridge on a country road and the driver out in the roadway beating the side of the truck with a stick. When asked what he is doing, the driver explains that his load is too heavy for the bridge and he is making the birds fly so as to lighten his load before proceeding.

This suggests the following puzzle. A cage with a bird in it, perched on a swing, weighs four pounds. Is the weight of the cage less if the bird is flying about in the cage instead of sitting on the swing? Ignoring the fact that if left in an airtight box for long the bird would die, would the answer be different if an airtight box were substituted for the cage?

95: Diophantine Equations

Equations are said to be diophantine if they can be solved in whole numbers. Mathematicians have devoted much time to the solution of such equations and one of the better known equations is

$$x^n + y^n = z^n + t^n$$

where x, y, z and t are all different integers, none of which can be zero.

When $n = 4$, the simplest known solution is
$$158^4 + 59^4 = 134^4 + 133^4 = 635318657$$
When $n = 3$, the simplest solution is
$$12^3 + 1^3 = 10^3 + 9^3 = 1729$$
What is the simplest solution when $n = 2$?

96: Crossing the Estuary

In still water I can row my dingy at 5 miles per hour. Last evening when I rowed across the mouth of the estuary from the Town Landing to my dock, it took me a quarter as long again to make the crossing as it does in still water. Assuming the flow of the tide is constant all the way across the mouth of the estuary and is at right angles to the line from the Town Landing to my dock, how fast was the tide flowing?

97: Colored Labels

Three intelligent men, A, B, and C, sit down to try out a test in logical reasoning. They are so arranged that each can see the color of a label which is either red or blue, attached to the hats worn by the other two but no one of them can see the color of the label attached to his own hat. They are told that at least one of the labels is red. If any one of them can logically deduce the color of the label on his hat, he is to declare it.

After a little time C, who has kept his eyes closed all the time and has not seen the label on any of the hats declares his label is red. How could he deduce this?

PUZZLERS 63

98: Find the Missing Digits

In the following long division X represents a digit and
the dividend

$$. \overset{\cdot}{X} X X X \overset{\cdot}{X}$$

is a recurring decimal with a recurring period of four. Can
you reconstruct the whole long division problem, given only
the single digit 3?

```
                  . x x x x x
        x x x )  x 3 x . x                (1)
                 x x x . x                (2)
                 x . x x x                (3)
                 . x x x                   (4)
                     x x x                 (5)
                     x x x                 (6)
                       x x x x            (7)
                         x x x            (8)
                         etc.
```

99: A Curious Walk

A man starting from a certain point walked 1 mile due
south. He then turned and walked one mile due east. He
turned again and walked one mile due north, when he
found he was exactly at his starting point. From where did
he start his walk?

There is a comparatively simple solution to this problem
and a more difficult solution. Can you find both?

100: Football Logic

My son who has been studying logic at school was trying to explain its principles to me. To illustrate his explanation he took the three statements:

(1) All my friends are on the football team.
(2) Some of my friends are not on the football team.
(3) Some, but not all, of my friends are on the football team.

At least one of these statements must be true.

(a) Which pair of statements might both be true or might both be false?
(b) Which pair of statements might both be false but cannot both be true?
(c) Which pair of statements cannot both be true and cannot both be false?

SOLUTIONS

1: Don't Spend It All at Once

If I spend all but $3, I must have $3 left.

2: Nine Boxes

So long as it is assumed that a change from one straight line to the next must be made at one of the boxes the solution is impossible, but, if the idea of continuing a straight line beyond the square of the boxes before changing direction is examined, a solution is easily found.

In the solution shown in Figure 1 the first line is drawn through the top three boxes and continued beyond the third box sufficiently far so that the second line can be drawn through the third box of the second row and the second box of the third row.

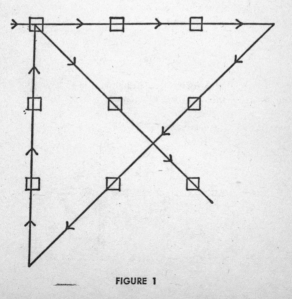

FIGURE 1

3: At the Five and Ten

We are told that each item was the same price. Let us assume each item cost x cents. We are also told that I bought as many items as the number of cents in the cost of each item. Therefore, I bought x items. If I had bought two items, I would have paid 2x cents in total; if I had bought 3 items, I would have paid 3x cents in total. Since I bought x items, I paid x times x or x^2 cents in total.

Now the total bill was 225 cents, hence $x^2 = 225$.

The square root of 225 can, of course, be obtained by looking it up in some tables, but we rarely have tables handy. Also, there is a method of calculating square roots, but when, as in this case, we know the answer must be a whole number, it is simplest to factorize the amount for which we want the square root.

Any number ending in 25, 50, 75 or 00 is a multiple of 25 or five times 5. Dividing 25 into 225 we have

$$225 = 9 . 25$$
$$= 3 . 3 . 5 . 5$$

The square root of 225 is, therefore, 3 . 5 or 15. Hence, I bought 15 articles for 15 cents each.

4: A Match Problem

In Figure 2 the former positions of the three repositioned matches are indicated by dotted lines.

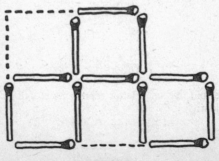

FIGURE 2

5: Hands of a Clock

It is tempting to give the "obvious" answer 12, but the true answer is 11, as will be found by counting the individual occasions.

1. Between 6:30 A.M. and 6:35 A.M.
2. Between 7:35 A.M. and 7:40 A.M.
3. Between 8:40 A.M. and 8:45 A.M.
4. Between 9:45 A.M. and 9:50 A.M.
5. Between 10:50 A.M. and 10:55 A.M.
6. At Noon.
7. Between 1:05 P.M. and 1:10 P.M.
8. Between 2:10 P.M. and 2:15 P.M.
9. Between 3:15 P.M. and 3:20 P.M.
10. Between 4:20 P.M. and 4:25 P.M.
11. Between 5:25 P.M. and 5:30 P.M.

6: Counting Squares

If the total length of the side of the figure is 4 inches, then counting the squares of each size we have:

½ inch x ½ inch	8 squares
1 inch x 1 inch	18 squares
2 inches x 2 inches	9 squares
3 inches x 3 inches	4 squares
4 inches x 4 inches	1 square
	40 squares

7: Letters for Digits

We are told that each letter represents a digit in the following problem:

$$
\begin{array}{r}
A\,B\,A \\
-\ C\,A \\
\hline
A\,B
\end{array}
$$

From this we deduce
$$AB + CA = ABA$$
Now, looking at the letters in the units position,
$$B + A = A$$
This is only possible if B = 0 (zero), and we have
$$A0 + CA = A0A$$
Looking at the letters in the tens and hundreds positions,
$$A + C = A0$$
Now A and C cannot be greater than 9, and since they are different, their sum cannot be greater than 17. Hence A0 cannot be greater than 17 and A must be 1.

Therefore, 1 + C = 10.

Giving C = 9 and the whole solution is

$$\begin{array}{r} 101 \\ -\ 91 \\ \hline 10 \end{array}$$

8: Which Games Do They Play?

The one who does not play tennis does not bowl and, also, he does not play golf. Therefore, he does not play any of the three games. Hence, the other two friends play all three games.

9: My Checking Account

If I write x checks a month, my present charge is
$$25 + 10x \text{ cents.}$$
Under the new arrangement I shall pay
$$50 + 8x \text{ cents.}$$
My saving per month is
$$25 + 10x - (50 + 8x)$$
$$\text{or } 2x - 25$$

If I am to make a saving, this must be positive and 2x must be greater than 25.

Dividing both items by 2
$$x \text{ must be greater than } 12\frac{1}{2}.$$

Hence, I must draw 13 or more checks a month to make a saving.

10: Four Word Problems

(1) DENY
(2) BOOKKEEPER
(3) DEEDED
(4) BETRAYAL

11: How Old Is My Daughter?

Let us assume my daughter is age x. We are told my daughter is twice as old as my son, so that my son must be age $\dfrac{x}{2}$. We are also told that I am twice as old as my daughter so my age is 2x. In 22 years time the ages will be

Person	Present age	Age 22 years hence
My daughter	x	x + 22
My son	$\dfrac{x}{2}$	$\dfrac{x}{2} + 22$
I	2x	2x + 22

Now in 22 years time, my son will be half my age. Hence,

$$\frac{x}{2} + 22 = \frac{1}{2}(2x + 22)$$

Multiplying both sides by 2

$$x + 44 = 2x + 22$$
$$\text{or} \qquad x = 22$$

My daughter is 22 years old.

12: Dice

Dice are always made with the numbers on opposite sides adding up to seven. One and six are on opposite sides, two and five are on opposite sides and three and four are on opposite sides.

Hence, the number on the side face down on the table is five.

13: Another Match Problem

The solution depends on the approximation to π, the ratio of the circumference of a circle to its diameter (see Figure 3).

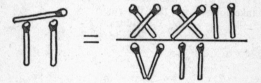

FIGURE 3

14: Some Series

(1) The first approach to any series problem is to calculate how much each term is greater (or less) than the previous term. We see that:

$$11 - \ 8 = \ 3$$
$$14 - 11 = \ 3$$
$$17 - 14 = \ 3$$
$$20 - 17 = \ 3$$
$$23 - 20 = \ 3$$

It is reasonable to assume that this rule will continue to hold and the next term will be

$$23 + 3 = 26$$

(2) In this series the differences between successive terms are:

$$9 - \ 6 = \ 3$$
$$18 - \ 9 = \ 9$$
$$21 - 18 = \ 3$$
$$42 - 21 = 21$$
$$45 - 42 = \ 3$$

The 2nd, 4th, and 6th terms are obtained by increasing the

SOLUTIONS 73

previous term by 3, but what is the rule for the 3rd and 5th terms? We soon notice that the 3rd term is twice the 2nd term and the 5th term is twice the 4th term.

It is reasonable to suppose, therefore, that even terms are obtained by adding 3 to the previous term and odd terms are obtained by doubling the previous term. Hence, the 7th term is 90.

(3) This problem is rather more complicated, but it should not take long to see that the rule is

subtract 3
divide by 3
add 3
subtract 3
divide by 3

and the 7th term will be obtained by adding 3, giving 4.

15: Can You?

This statement was made by a salmon fisherman who was asked what he did with all the fish he caught.

16: The Striking Clock

The strike I heard was either one o'clock or some half hour. If, after another half hour I hear two or more strikes, I know what hour it is, but, if I again hear one strike, I may have heard successively 12:30 A.M. and 1 o'clock or 1 o'clock and 1:30 A.M. After another half hour I either hear 1 strike (1:30 A.M.) or 2 strikes (2 o'clock). I may, therefore, have to lie awake a whole hour before I can be sure of the exact time.

17: Ages

If Bill is age X, Jim is $30 - X$. In 14 years Jim will be $30 - X + 14 = 44 - X$. This must equal three times Bill's age or $3X$.

$$\therefore \ 44 - X = 3X$$
$$\text{or} \qquad 4X = 44$$

Bill is 11 and Jim is 19.

18: Relations

(1) Only dead men have widows.
(2) I am "this man."
(3) Jill is Jean's mother.

19: Paper Cutting

If we draw the original square, the circle of paper cut from it and the final smaller square, and make the sides of the second square at 45° to the sides of the original square, we have the diagram shown in Figure 4.

Set out in this way, we see that the area of triangle EHO equals one-half the area of the square AEOH and hence the square remaining after the two cuttings, EFGH, is half the original piece of paper, ABCD. One-half of the original square of paper is cut off and thrown away.

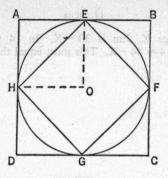

FIGURE 4

20: Skiing

It is very tempting to say that, if I go up at 5 miles an hour and come down at 25 miles an hour, my average speed is 15 miles an hour. If this reasoning were sound, we could say that if I went up at zero miles an hour (if, in fact, I never went up at all) my average speed would be $\dfrac{0 + 25}{2}$ or 12½ miles an hour. Trick questions of this nature are common in mathematical tests.

Let us assume that the length of the ski slope is 1 mile. Then it would take me ⅕ of an hour to go up at 5 miles an hour and ¹⁄₂₅ of an hour to come down at 25 miles an hour. This gives the total time for the 2 mile round trip of

$$\frac{1}{5} + \frac{1}{25} = \frac{6}{25} \text{ of an hour}$$

to travel 2 miles, and the average speed is

$$2 \times \frac{25}{6} = 8\frac{1}{3} \text{ miles an hour.}$$

We do not, of course, know that the slope is 1 mile long.

Let us assume it is d miles long.
   Then the time to go up the slope is

$$\frac{d}{5} \text{ hours}$$

The time to come down the slope is

$$\frac{d}{25} \text{ hours}$$

This gives a total time of

$$\frac{d}{5} + \frac{d}{25} = \frac{6d}{25} \text{ hours}$$

from 2d miles, and the average speed is

$$2d \times \frac{25}{6d} = 8\frac{1}{3} \text{ miles an hour.}$$

21: School Notes

If   6 boys fill 6 notebooks in 6 weeks,
      12 boys fill 12 notebooks in 6 weeks,
and 12 boys fill 24 notebooks in 12 weeks;
If   4 girls fill 4 notebooks in 4 weeks,
      12 girls fill 12 notebooks in 4 weeks,
and 12 girls fill 36 notebooks in 12 weeks;
Hence 12 girls and 12 boys fill 24 + 36 = 60 notebooks in
      12 weeks.

22: A Different Type of Maze

We note first that when DD are joined, there is only one route (above the upper D) from the left side of the grid to the right. Clearly only one of the two lines BB and CC can take this route. Hence, DD must pass to the left of both C's, and BB must pass above the upper D. Proceeding in this manner, we establish the only possible solution (see Figure 5).

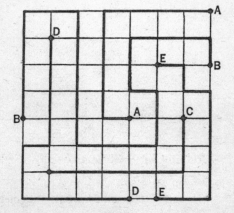

FIGURE 5

78 SOLUTIONS

23: Three Friends

We can number the three pieces of information:
(1) Thomas is a bachelor.
(2) Richard earns less than the youngest of the three.
(3) The oldest of the three earns most but has the cost of putting his son through college.

From (3) the oldest is not a bachelor and, hence, from (1), is not Thomas. From (3) the oldest earns the most and, therefore, from (2) cannot be Richard. Hence the oldest must be John. From (2) Richard is not the youngest and so Thomas must be the youngest.

The full information is set out below:
Oldest—John—Earns Most—Putting son through college
Middle—Richard—Earns Least
Youngest—Thomas—Bachelor
John is the oldest, Thomas the youngest.

24: A Teen-age Club

Let us assume the number of boys now in the club is x. Since there is now one boy for each five girls, the present membership of the club is

Boys	Girls
x	5x

Prior to this, 45 boys moved out because they were unhappy with the setup. Prior to their withdrawal, there were

Boys	Girls
x + 45	5x

At this time there were two boys to each girl so that
$$x + 45 = 10x$$
$$\text{Therefore} \quad 9x = 45$$
$$\text{or} \quad x = 5$$

giving:

Boys	Girls
50	25

Between the outing and the time when there were 50 boys and 25 girls, 15 girls withdrew so that there were $25 + 15 = 40$ girls at the time of the outing.

25: The Two Wrestlers

Lord John and his wife Betty, a lady wrestler, had a child. Unfortunately they separated and finally were divorced, although they remained friends. Betty later married Mr. Jones.

26: Simple Geometry

Since OC is 5 units long and CD 1 unit long, the radius of the circle is 6 units.

Since ABCO is a parallelogram, its diagonals are equal. Therefore, AC = BO = 6 units (the radius of the circle). (See Figure 6.)

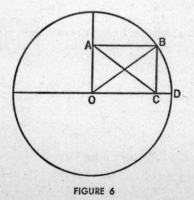

FIGURE 6

27: Tom, Dick and Harry

For each cent Harry spends, Dick spends 2 cents and Tom 4 cents. Therefore, for each cent Harry spends,

Dick spends 1 more cent than Harry,
Tom spends 3 more cents than Harry,
Tom spends 2 more cents than Dick.

However many cents Harry spends, Tom's excess spending over Harry's will be a multiple of 3 cents and Tom's excess spending over Dick's will be a multiple of 2 cents. Since Smith's excess spending over Robinson is $12.65 which is not a multiple of 2 or 3 cents, Smith must be Dick and Robinson must be Harry. Hence the names are:

Tom Jones
Dick Smith
Harry Robinson

28: Going to Town

Since I went to the Farmer's Market I must have gone to town on Monday, Wednesday or Saturday. I could not have had a haircut on Monday, nor could I have gone to the bank on Saturday. Therefore, I went to town on Wednesday.

29: No Change

In order to pay the exact price for any item from 1 cent to 4 cents, I must have at least 4 cents. Trial shows that the least total number of coins to pay the exact price for any item from

1 cent up to and including 1 dollar is

> 4 cents
> 1 nickel
> 2 dimes
> 1 quarter
> 1 half dollar
> —
> making 9 coins in all

It should be noted that the same solution, but with 2 nickels and 1 dime, will not pay for an item of 1 dollar.

The fewest number of coins I could have in my pocket is 9.

30: My Four Children

We are told Jean is 1 and hence John, who is four times Jean's age, is 4. Now Joan is either three times John's age, that is 3, or three times Jean's age, that is 12.

Bill cannot be twice as old as Jean because this would make him the third oldest; nor can he be twice as old as Joan because this would make him the oldest. Hence, Bill is twice as old as John and is 8 years old, and Joan must be 12.

The ages are:

> Jean   1
> John   4
> Bill   8
> Joan 12

Bill is 8 years old.

31: Crossing the Line

As long as you start in one of the two areas with an odd number of sides (shaded in Figure 7) there is no difficulty. Starting in any other area the problem is impossible.

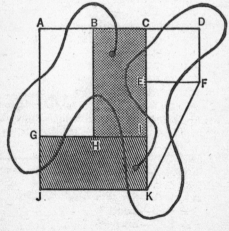

FIGURE 7

32: The Collectors

Mr. Smith has clearly met Mr. Brown and Mr. Jones, hence he cannot be the lawyer or the doctor, who have never met. Hence, Mr. Smith is the banker. A "hallmark" appears on many pieces of old silver and so Mr. Jones is not the lawyer. These two pieces of information establish that

> Mr. Brown is the lawyer.
> Mr. Smith is the banker.
> Mr. Jones is the doctor.

33: Palindromes

The eight common four-letter palindromes are:

> A N N A—Indian coin
> B O O B—simpleton
> D E E D—brave act
> N O O N—midday
> P E E P—look furtively
> P O O P—stern of ship
> S E E S—discerns with the eyes
> T O O T—sound of horn

Ma'am is not acceptable because it is a slang word.

There are some less usual four-letter palindromes which may be found in some dictionaries.

> A B B A—Coptic divine
> A K K A—a pigmie people of the Congo
> A L L A—in the manner of
> A M M A—Syrian abbess
> D O O D—camel
> E S S E—essential being
> K E E K—peep

34: Simple Algebra

There was nothing wrong as far as the line
$$(x + y)(x - y) = y(x - y)$$
If we substitute the values of x and y we have
$$2 \times 0 = 1 \times 0$$
       or
$$0 = 0$$
However, when we divide both sides by $(x - y)$, we break a fundamental rule of mathematics that we cannot divide out by a fraction which is equal to zero.

35: Letter Addition

Numbering the columns for reference, we have:

(1)	(2)	(3)	(4)
	A	B	C
		A	B
		A	A
D	E	E	A

The maximum which can be carried from the sum of the three digits in column (3) to column (2) is 2. Since D and E cannot represent the same digits, the only possible values for D and E are 1 and 0 respectively and A must be 8 or 9.

Trying $A = 9$ we note that B must be at least 2 (since $D = 1$ and $E = 0$) and hence the sum must be at least

$$
\begin{array}{ccc}
9 & 2 & ? \\
9 & ? & \\
9 & 9 & \\
\hline
\end{array}
$$

which adds to more than 1100. This is impossible because $E = 0$ and hence $A = 8$.

This gives

$$
\begin{array}{cccc}
 & 8 & 3 & 7 \\
 &   & 8 & 3 \\
 &   & 8 & 8 \\
\hline
1 & 0 & 0 & 8 \\
\end{array}
$$

which is the only possible solution.

SOLUTIONS   85

36: The Round Window

Since there are eight outer panes, each of which is to have
the same area as the inner pane, the area of the whole window
must be 9 times the area of the inner pane. Now the area of
a circle is proportional to the square of its diameter; hence if
the area of the whole window is 9 times that of the inner pane,
the diameter of the whole window is 3 times the diameter of
the inner pane, or 6 feet. Hence, the spokes should be 2 feet
long or 24 inches.

37: Fencing the Yard

Mr. Brown will require 25 sections for one frontage and
24 for the other, so the number of rails required is 3 x 49 = 147
rails. The number of posts required will be 26 for the side
without the driveway and also 26 for the side with the driveway since the gap for the driveway does not save any posts.
It must be noted that two posts will be required at the corner
where the two sides meet since the rails can go through the
posts at one angle only.

Hence, the answer is 147 rails and 52 posts.

38: The Newlyweds

Joan, whose husband is very short, cannot be married to
Bill who is a star basketball player. Nor can Joan, who is a
keen diver, be married to Dick whose wife does not swim.
Therefore, Joan must be married to the only other man, John.

Since Maryann is Dick's sister, they cannot be married and
since Dick is not married to Joan, he must be married to
Carolyn.

The couples are:

> John and Joan
> Dick and Carolyn
> Bill and Maryann

39: Four Triangles

First, place three sticks to form an equal-sided triangle lying on a table (see Figure 8).

Then place one end of each of the three remaining sticks at the points A, B, and C respectively and hold the other ends together at a point, O, immediately above the center of the triangle ABC. This makes four equal-sided triangles, ABC, OAB, OAC and OBC (see Figure 9).

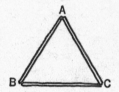

FIGURE 8

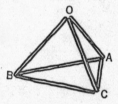

FIGURE 9

40: Keeping Account

Adding up the amount he spent we see he did spend the whole 50 cents and, therefore, he did not lose a cent. However, there is no reason why the sum of the money left after each purchase should add up to the original sum of 50 cents. If he had purchased two drawing books for 25 cents each, his "account" would be

		Money Left
Received	50 cents	
Drawing Book	25 cents	25 cents
Drawing Book	25 cents	..
		——
		25 cents

If he had purchased 5 bags of candy at 10 cents each, his "account" would be

		Money Left
Received	50 cents	
Candy	10 cents	40 cents
Candy	10 cents	30 cents
Candy	10 cents	20 cents
Candy	10 cents	10 cents
Candy	10 cents	..
		——
		$1.00

My young son did not lose a cent, but he had added up his money left after each purchase and found the total was one cent less than the amount with which he had started.

41: Children's Party

Five different-colored dresses are mentioned so that each girl wore a different color. Sheila raced with the girl in green against the girl in yellow so she wore neither of these colors. Betty wore blue and Ethel red, hence Sheila must have worn brown. Marge, therefore, did not wear brown. Betty and Ethel were in blue and red, hence Marge was in green. Therefore, the fifth girl, who must be Jane, wore yellow.

Jane wore yellow.
Our child liked Sheila best.

42: Change for a Dollar

There are eight possible ways of making change under the conditions prescribed.

(a) 1 half-dollar, 1 quarter, 2 dimes, 1 nickel
(b) 1 half-dollar, 1 quarter, 1 dime, 3 nickels
(c) 1 half-dollar, 4 dimes, 2 nickels
(d) 1 half-dollar, 3 dimes, 4 nickels
(e) 3 quarters, 2 dimes, 1 nickel
(f) 3 quarters, 1 dime, 3 nickels
(g) 2 quarters, 4 dimes, 2 nickels
(h) 2 quarters, 3 dimes, 4 nickels

The cashier can make change in eight ways.

43: Earning a Living

At first glance it would seem that A's salary increase of $520 per annum is much better than B's increase of $130 each half year. However, B's increase is an increase in his *half yearly salary*. B will receive $2,600 in his first half year and $2,600 + $130 = $2,730 in his second half year and $2,730 + $130 = $2,860 in his third half year. Therefore, in the first half of the second year B will be paid $2,860 which represents an annual rate of pay of $5,720. This is equal to A's $5,200 + $520 = $5,720. In fact, B will always receive the same as A in the first half of each year and $130 more than A in the second half of each year. We can see this more clearly if we set out how much each receives each half year.

Half Year	A Receives	B Receives
1	$2,600	$2,600
2	2,600	2,730
3	2,860	2,860
4	2,860	2,990
5	3,120	3,120
6	3,120	3,250

etc.

We see that for the first six months of each year A and B receive identical sums, but for the second six months of each year B receives more than A. Hence, if everything else is equal, B is offered the better contract.

44: Can You Thread the Maze?

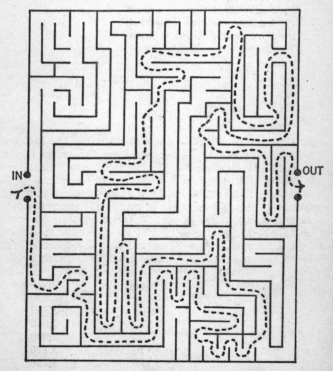

FIGURE 10

45: Four Men

Since Mr. Baker is a cable car driver, he must live in San Francisco, and since Mr. Davis is on an embassy staff, he must live in Washington. Since Mr. Davis lives closer to Mr. Allen than he does to the other two men, Mr. Allen must live in Boston.

Hence, we have

Mr. Allen lives in Boston.
Mr. Baker lives in San Francisco.
Mr. Campbell lives in Chicago.
Mr. Davis lives in Washington.

46: Do You Know?

(1) Although the Pacific Ocean lies to the west of the Atlantic Ocean you travel from west to east when actually passing through the canal from the Atlantic to the Pacific.
(2) Windsor, Canada, is almost due south of Detroit.
(3) Most northerly—Alaska
Most easterly—Maine
Most southerly—Hawaii
Most westerly—Alaska

47: Professor Cubit's Walk

Indicate the five areas of the town by A, B, C, D, and E in the town plan as shown in Figure 11. We see that three crosswalks end on A, four on B, six on C, three on D and two on E. If Professor Cubit is to cross each crosswalk once and only once, he must have started in an area with an odd number of crosswalks from it and ended in an area with an odd number of crosswalks to it. Since Professor Cubit's house was south of the chapel, it must be in area D and the chapel must be in area A. Hence, Professor Cubit's little house was on the east side of Elm Street.

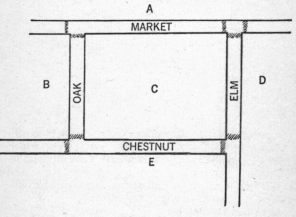

FIGURE 11

48: Selling Appliances

Since John made a 25% profit on one appliance and a 20% loss on the other, it is tempting to say he made a profit over all. This is not so. He estimated the washer was worth $40 and a profit of 25% gave him $50. He estimated the dryer was worth $62.50 and a loss of 20% gave him $50. Hence, he estimated the two pieces of equipment were worth $102.50 but then he sold them for only $100, suffering a small loss from his estimate.

49: A Dinner Party

Numbering the ten places around the table 1 to 10 as shown in Figure 12, if I take the head of the table (1), my wife will sit at (6), Jean will be at (10), Tom at (5), and Janet at (2).

Now my wife will not have Jack next to her so he must be at (9), because (3) would place him next to his wife. Since Maryann is next to Jack, she must be at (8); then Howard must be at (7), Bill at (3), and Lois at (4). (See Figure 13)

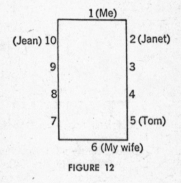

FIGURE 12

FIGURE 13

50: Sunday School Picnic

Since there are no odd cents in the sum collected, the number of children must have been a multiple of ten. If 60 children attended, the total receipts would be 60 cents plus at least 40 times 30 cents, the minimum charge for a grownup. This is more than $10. Less than 60 children would produce a still larger sum. Hence, the number of children must be 70, 80 or 90. 90 children will only leave 10 grownups who cannot pay more than $5, making a total less than $10. Hence, the number of children must be 70 or 80. Simple trial soon shows the only answer to be

80 children at 1 cent	=	.80
16 men at 50 cents	=	8.00
4 women at 30 cents	=	1.20
100		$10.00

51: Old Friend Hypotenuse

If ABC is a right angle triangle with BC the hypotenuse, the rectangle formed by ABCD in Figure 14 will have two diagonals, AD and BC, meeting at O. O is the mid point of both BC and AD, and hence the length AO must be equal to one-half BC.

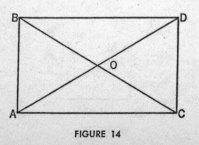

FIGURE 14

52: What Is Wrong?

(1) Legend tells us that Leander swam the Hellespont each night to visit Hero, the priestess of Aphrodite, but if he had swum it seven times a day he would have had to sleep on opposite sides each night.

(2) Astronauts circle the globe about once every 90 minutes, hence, they can see a sunset about every 90 minutes. There is no reason to suppose they get most tired at intervals of this frequency.

(3) Although the Pilgrim Fathers landed near Plymouth Rock, the Stars and Stripes was not introduced until the Revolution many years after they arrived.

(4) Although the Romans were occupying Britain in 55 B.C., no coin could be dated 55 B.C. since B.C. is short for "Before Christ" and in 55 B.C. no one knew when Christ would be born.

53: Dominoes on a Board

The use of a chessman to block out the middle square gives the clue to the solution of this problem. If the board is marked out as a chess board with alternate black and white squares, with the middle square black, we find that there are 32 white squares and 30 black squares (not counting the middle square). Now a domino however placed will cover one white square and one black square and hence having placed 30 dominoes we shall always be left with 2 white squares which cannot possibly be covered by a single domino. Hence, there is no possible solution to the problem.

54: Winning at Chess

While Mark was not an expert chess player, obviously some-one had put him up to a trick to beat me.

I opened by making a usual move of the King's Pawn with white on Board A. Mark proceeded to make the identical opening with white on Board B. It was now my turn to play on Board B and I made a usual black response. Mark made the identical response with black on Board A. I now made an un-usual Knight's move with white on Board A and Mark made the same unusual move with white on Board B. Then the penny dropped. I realized that Mark had set a clever trap for me. Every move I made on either board would be duplicated by Mark on the other board so that the two games would always be identical. If I won on Board A, Mark would win on Board B. If I had a draw on Board A, Mark would draw on Board B. It seemed a waste of time to play any further, so I resigned and gave Mark his bicycle.

55: Do You Know Your Calendar?

(1) 9 years. A.D. 1 follows immediately after 1 B.C.
(2) The Julian Calendar which was introduced by Julius Caesar provided that every fourth year was a leap year of 366 days compared with the ordinary year of 365 days. Hence, the average year was assumed to be 365¼ days. This is about 11 minutes too long. The cumulative error became sufficiently large by the sixteenth century that a correction was necessary. This was achieved by the Gregorian Calendar introduced by Pope Gregory XIII in Italy in 1582 which provided that cen-tury years do not count as leap years unless divisible by 400. To correct for the accumulated error October 4, 1582 was followed immediately by October 15, ten days thus being

missed out. England did not adopt the new calendar until 1752 when September 2 was followed by September 14 with the loss of eleven days.

(3) In a normal year March 1 is the sixtieth day of the year. In a leap year it is the sixty-first. As explained above, the year A.D. 2000 will be a leap year and the correct answer is 61.

56: Which Is the Even Way?

(See Figure 15.)

A few trials suggest that all routes from A to B pass through an odd number of towns. If we go along the top of the plan we pass through 3 towns. If we go the long way round the bottom we pass through 15 towns. We should next note that area AVWXYZ has six towns on its perimeter. If we go from A to W one way we go through 1 town (V) and the other way we go through 3 towns (Z, Y and X). We learn from this that for an even-sided area, it does not matter which way around we go; we shall not change the number of towns on the total route from odd to even or from even to odd. We now start to look for areas with an odd number of towns on their perimeter and we find there are two (shaded in Figure 15). To find a route through an even number of towns we must pass around one shaded area but not the other. Since the two shaded areas meet at C, the even way from A to B must pass through C, either from side to side or from top to bottom. With this information it does not take long to find the correct route, which passes through 12 towns.

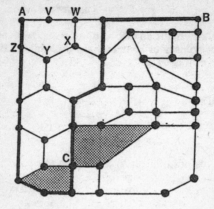

FIGURE 15

57: Suburban Commuting

The official was correct when he said that the trains to any individual station would be half as frequent, but he was incorrect when he claimed there would be no speedup of the journey. Even if it takes twice as long to unload twice as many passengers at each stop, there will be a speeding up because the train will have to slow down to stop only half the number of times and gain speed from start half the number of times.

58: For Stamp Collectors

For the mathematician the solution is the well-known formula for the number of combinations of 5 things taken 3 at a time. This is expressed as

$$\binom{5}{3}$$

and is equal to

$$\frac{5!}{3! \ 2!} = \frac{5.4.3.2.1}{(3.2.1)\ (2.1)} = 10$$

However, it is not difficult to obtain the solution of the problem without any knowledge of these formulae. All we need to do is to represent the five stamps by the letters A, B, C, D and E and to write down all possible combinations in dictionary order. The use of dictionary order in finding solutions to a problem of this kind avoids the danger of using the same combination twice and makes it easy to be sure all combinations have been used.

The possible combinations are:

A B C	A D E
A B D	B C D
A B E	B C E
A C D	B D E
A C E	C D E

giving 10 possible combinations.

59: The Flagpole

If A is the edge of the door, B is the flagpole and C is myself, ABC will be in a straight line. Let X be the center of the doorway and Y the center of the Mall from where I stand. The triangles BAX and BCY are similar and hence the ratio BX to BY is equal to the ratio of AX to CY. Now AX is 5 feet and CY is 40 feet so that the ratio is 5/40 or 1/8.

Therefore,

$$BX = \tfrac{1}{8} \ BY$$
$$= \tfrac{1}{8} \ 600 \text{ yards,}$$
$$\text{or} \qquad 75 \text{ yards,}$$

The flagpole is 75 yards from the main doorway. (See Figure 16.)

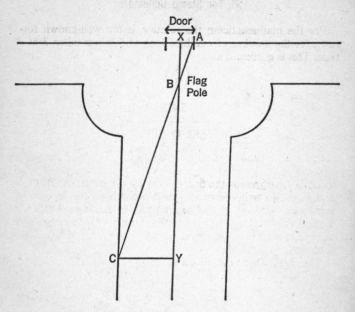

FIGURE 16

60: Shingles and Apples

This is a common trap in mathematical tests. The charge for the apples should be 33⅓ cents for large apples and 20 cents for smaller apples, so the average charge per apple should be

$$\frac{33\frac{1}{3} + 20}{2} = 26\frac{2}{3} \text{ cents}$$

and not 25 cents, which the boy collected. If the 60 apples had been sold for 26⅔ cents each, the boy would have received

$$60 \times 26\frac{2}{3} \text{ cents or } \$16.$$

The son was charging too little for the apples and the dollar went to the customers.

61: An Easy Cross-Number Problem

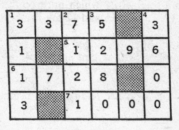

FIGURE 17

62: Our Bank Staff

Since Mr. Brown is taller than the auditor or the teller, he can be neither of these two. Since Mr. Smith is older than the auditor, he cannot be the auditor, and since Mr. Foster lunches with the auditor and the teller, he can be neither of these. Since none of Mr. Brown, Mr. Smith or Mr. Foster can be the auditor, he must be Mr. Jones. Hence, the teller, who cannot be Mr. Brown, Mr. Foster, or Mr. Jones must be Mr. Smith.

Since the manager lunches alone, he cannot be Mr. Foster so he must be Mr. Brown and we have

> Mr. Smith—teller
> Mr. Brown—manager
> Mr. Jones—auditor
> Mr. Foster—accountant

The references to basketball and bridge are red herrings.

63: Getting Soft Drinks

The children's ages are 4, 5, 6, 7, 8, 9, 10, 11, 12, 13. The only two of these numbers which can add up to 10 is 4 and 6. Hence, 4 and 6 are brothers. The total of 23 can be obtained by adding 10 and 13, or 11 and 12. In the former case we cannot obtain a total of 22 which must be the sum of 9 and 13 or 10 and 12. Hence, 11 and 12 are brothers and 9 and 13 are brothers.

This leaves the four boys aged 5, 7, 8 and 10. Since two of these are brothers with a joint age of 13 and the other two are brothers with a joint age of 17, 5 and 8 must be brothers and 7 and 10 must be brothers.

Since one of my sons is 7 years old, his brother must be 10.

64: Changing Figures

(1) Changing from A to B shortens vertical distances and leaves horizontal distances unchanged and, hence, Y is the correct solution.
(2) Changing from A to B involves a 90° counterclockwise turn and, hence, X is the correct solution.
(3) Changing from A to B involves a 90° counterclockwise turn for the top half and an independent 90° clockwise turn for the bottom half. Since C consists of a circle and a square, both of which are unaffected by such turns, Z is the correct solution.

65: Four Readers

The reference to "the wife with blue eyes" indicates that only one of the wives has blue eyes, hence, one of the men must have blue eyes.

Since Mr. Collins has brown eyes, Mr. Webster must have blue eyes.

The wife who does not have blue eyes cannot like history best because one of the men likes it best; she cannot like biography best because one of the two with blue eyes likes it best and she cannot like adventure stories best because the blue eyed wife likes these best. Hence, she must like detective stories best.

We can plot this information, and the other direct information given, using *Yes* for preference and *No* for non-preference.

	Mr. Webster (Blue eyes)	Mr. Collins (Brown eyes)	Blue eyed wife	Wife who does not have blue eyes
History				No
Biography		No		No
Detective Novels				Yes
Adventure Stories			Yes	No

Since each has a different preference, "Yes" must appear once and once only in every line and column. Hence, we can add "No" in the blank spaces in the two bottom lines and in the third column.

	Mr. Webster (Blue eyes)	Mr. Collins (Brown eyes)	Blue eyed wife	Wife who does not have blue eyes
History			No	No
Biography		No	No	No
Detective Novels	No	No	No	Yes
Adventure Stories	No	No	Yes	No

We then see that Mr. Webster must prefer biography and Mr. Collins, history.

Since the husband with the blue eyed wife likes history best, Mrs. Collins is blue eyed and prefers adventure stories.

66: Friday the Thirteenth

There are twelve months in the year of 365¼ (average) days, so that the thirteenth day of the month occurs once in

$$\frac{365¼}{12} \text{ days}$$

The day of the week is equally likely to be any one of seven, hence, Friday the thirteenth occurs on the average, once in

$$\frac{365¼}{12} \times 7 = \frac{2556¾}{12} \text{ days}$$

$$= 213 \text{ days}$$

Hence, on the average, Friday the thirteenth occurs once every 213 days.

67: The Planets

(2) is a reasonably correct statement of the facts. The planets, which revolve around the sun, are smaller but much nearer the earth than are the stars. The stars are so far away from the earth that they appear fixed in position, despite their actual motion. Planets are proportionately nearer the earth so that their motion is apparent in relation to the stars. All stars and planets appear to twinkle at times because of changes in the earth's atmosphere.

68: Simple Topology

Although it looks difficult to get the cup off the string, it is actually very easy. Take the center point of the loop, where it passes behind the two lines on which the cup hangs and pull on it until you have a loop large enough to pull around the cup. Pull the loop around the cup, from the back forward, and the cup will be disconnected from the string.

69: Star Polygons

Let x be the angle DAC (see Figure 18). The line AD must
be turned through the angle x to bring it to AC. AC must be
turned through x again to bring it to EC. Again EC must be
turned through x to bring it to EB. Proceeding in this manner
we find that AD must be turned through the angle x five times
to bring it back to itself, but in the process AD has acquired
opposite sense, so that A is now where D was and D is now
where A was. Hence, the line AD has been turned through
180°. From this we calculate $5x = 180°$ or $x = 36°$.

The angles at the points of the star are 36°.

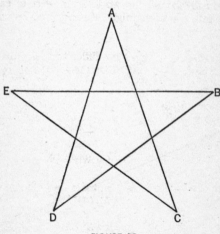

FIGURE 18

70: Is It Possible?

(1) The theory of relativity tells us that no particle or wave, or other means of transmitting information, can travel faster than the speed of light. Since light travels 186,000 miles a second, this should be as fast as anyone could want.

(2) There have been many cases where a patient's heart has stopped beating, but he has been restored to life by massaging the muscles of the heart.

(3) Water often travels uphill in pipes. Thus, water must travel up the pipe to a second floor bathroom.

(4) Occasionally in circus acts a bicycle will be ridden on a track which loops-the-loop. The centrifugal force due to rotation will make the cyclist ride upside down at the top of the loop.

(5) If you sail round the world from west to east and you cross the date line at midnight, the time will be put back one day and you will live through the same day (as defined by the date) twice.

(6) Fast sailing craft have no difficulty when the wind is on the quarter in traveling faster than the wind.

71: Birthday Wishes

Number each column in the puzzle for reference, thus

```
      (1) (2) (3) (4) (5)
       H   A   P   P   Y
       B   I   R   T   H
               D   A   Y
      ─────────────────────
       D   T   A   T   H
       D   A   D   D   Y
      ─────────────────────
       I   T   X   H   I
```

From the top half of column (5), Y must be equal to 0 or 5, the bottom half of the column shows Y does not equal 0, hence $Y = 5$.

From the bottom half of (1) D must be 4 or less (since 2D is less than 10) and from the top half of (1) D must be at least 3 and H and B must be 1, 2 or 3.

Putting H equal to 1, 2 or 3 in turn we have

H	I	D	T	A
—	from (5)	from (1)	from (4)	from (1) & (2)
1	6	3	8	0
2	7	3	9	9
3	8	4	9	0

H = 2 is impossible because this makes T and A both 9 and H = 3 is impossible because this makes P = 9 (from (4)) which is the same as T. Hence, H = 1 and the full solution is

```
        1 0 9 9 5
        2 6 7 8 1
            3 0 5
        ---------
        3 8 0 8 1
        3 0 3 3 5
        ---------
        6 8 4 1 6
        ---------
```

72: Paying Bills

Since the dollars in the drugstore bill were exactly equal to the cents in the hardware bill and the cents in the drugstore bill were exactly equal to the dollars in the hardware bill, the total of the two bills must have the same number of dollars as cents.

Since all four bills total $55.25 and the other two bills were in exact dollars, the total of the drugstore and the hardware bills must be $25.25. The doctor's and dentist's bills must total the balance of $30.00.

Now the doctor's bill was half as much again as the dentist's bill so that if the dentist's bill was 2x dollars and the doctor's bill was 3x dollars, therefore 5x = 30 and the dentist's bill was $12.00 and the doctor's, $18.00.

Since the dentist's bill was the smallest, both the drugstore bill and the hardware bill must be greater than $12.00. Hence, these two bills must be $12.13 and $13.12. Since the drugstore bill was the second smallest, this must be $12.13.

The bills were:

Doctor	$18.00
Hardware	13.12
Drugstore	12.13
Dentist	12.00
	$55.25

73: Meeting Uncle William

If I am home 10 minutes late I must have driven for 5 minutes more before I picked up Uncle William. Hence, I picked him up 5 minutes later than usual. In 5 minutes I drive $(36 \div 12)$ miles which is 3 miles. Hence, I picked him up 3 miles nearer his home, 5 minutes later than usual. Uncle William would have walked the 3 miles in 1 hour. He must have watched the tree planting for 1 hour and 5 minutes.

74: Heads and Tails

It is tempting to say that since the chance of a head when a single coin is tossed is a half, the chance of two heads out of four coins tossed is a half. This is not so.

Each of the four coins is equally likely to fall head or tail so that there are $2 \times 2 \times 2 \times 2 = 16$ equally likely results of tossing the four coins at once. These can be readily written down:

(1) H H H H		(9) T H H H
(2) H H H T		(10) T H H T
(3) H H T H		(11) T H T H
(4) H H T T		(12) T H T T
(5) H T H H		(13) T T H H
(6) H T H T		(14) T T H T
(7) H T T H		(15) T T T H
(8) H T T T		(16) T T T T

Numbers 4, 6, 7, 10, 11 and 13 are the only cases where exactly two heads and two tails occur. Hence, two heads and two tails may be expected 6 times in 16 throws and the probability of them occurring is ⅜.

75: The Moon

(1) Since the moon rises one hour later each day, the last quarter of the moon is not visible in the evening, hence, I must see the first quarter.

(2) Full moon occurs approximately once every 28 days or thirteen times a year.

(3) At the time of a total eclipse of the sun, a person on the earth observes that the moon almost exactly covers the sun.

Hence, the ratio of m (the diameter of the moon) to S (the diameter of the sun) is equal to the ratio of d (the distance of the moon) to D (the distance of the sun.)

$$\frac{m}{S} = \frac{d}{D}$$

We are given that S = 860,000 miles, D = 93,000,000 miles and d = 240,000 miles. Hence,

$$m = \frac{240,000}{93,000,000} \times 860,000 \text{ miles}$$

$$= 2,200 \text{ miles approximately}$$

The actual diameter of the moon is 2,160 miles. (See Figure 19)

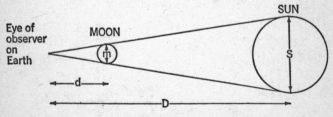

FIGURE 19

76: Missing Digits

Because the dividend is a whole number, the digits brought down for the second line of division (4) must be zero, and since there is no remainder, the last line (5) must also end in two zeros. (See Figure 20a)

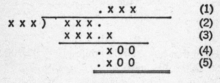

FIGURE 20a

The divisor must be an exact multiple of line (3) and line (5). Since line (3) cannot end in a zero and line (5) ends in two zeros, the divisor must end in 25 or 75, and the last digit of line (3) must be 5. Hence, line (5) is 500 and the divisor is 125. The whole solution is shown in Figure 20b.

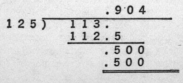

FIGURE 20b

77: An Unusual Series

Each term consists of the first digit of the preceding term multiplied by the second digit of the same term. Thus,

$$49 = 7 \times 7$$
$$36 = 4 \times 9$$
$$18 = 3 \times 6$$

Hence, the fifth term is $1 \times 8 = 8$.

78: Do You Know Your United States?

(1)   Lake Michigan (Lake Superior is partly in Canada).
(2)   Miami
(3)   Tennessee has common borders with

Virginia	Mississippi
North Carolina	Arkansas
Georgia	Missouri
Alabama	Kentucky

Missouri has common borders with

Iowa	Arkansas
Illinois	Oklahoma
Kentucky	Kansas
Tennessee	Nebraska

(4)   Colorado and Wyoming.
(5)   A small portion of Minnesota called Northwest Angle.

79: Climbing the Mountain

Bob was most correct when he stated that the cold was due to the rarefied atmosphere. While it is true that the sun's rays are stronger at greater heights and that winds have a cooling effect and the greater the height the stronger the winds, the main reason for the lower temperature at greater heights is the rarefied atmosphere. With fewer molecules per cubic inch, fewer molecules bombard us each second and less heat is transmitted to us by the surrounding body of air.

80: Is the Rope Knotted?

We can assume without loss of completeness that at A the rope going from top left to bottom right is on top. (If it is the other way a mirror solution is produced which does not alter the probability.) (See Figure 21)

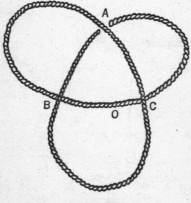

FIGURE 21

Then we have four equal possibilities. The segment BOC can be either on top or underneath at each of the points B and C.

Segment BOC

At B	At C	The rope is
On top	On top	Not knotted
On top	Under	Not knotted
Under	On top	Knotted
Under	Under	Not knotted

Hence the chance that the rope is knotted is 1/4.

81: The Two Rugs

The 10 foot by 10 foot rug must be cut as shown in Figure 22, each step being 2 feet long and 1 foot broad.

This gives two odd-shaped pieces. (See Figure 23)

If we move the right-hand piece up one foot and bring the two pieces together, a gap will be left in the middle which can be exactly filled by the 8 foot by 1 foot strip, which is shaded in Figure 24.

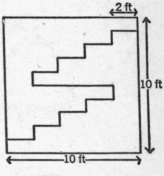

FIGURE 22

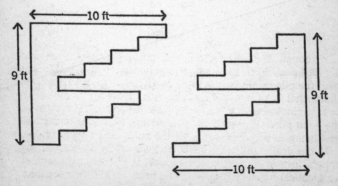

FIGURE 23

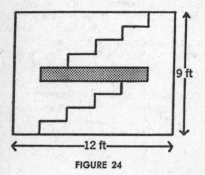

FIGURE 24

82: Lost Deal

Although Professor Cubit did not know where he had stopped dealing, he did know where he had started, which was with the pile on his immediate left. If he deals *backward* from there, that is to say, if he starts with his own pile and deals counterclockwise, the cards will be distributed correctly to the four piles. It should be pointed out that such a method of dealing is not allowed under the rules of whist or bridge.

If the dealer not only deals backward but deals from the bottom instead of the top of the pack, the players will receive the identical hands they would have been dealt if the telephone had never rung.

83: Little League Baseball

Let us assume there were x little league clubs. Then each club will play (x - 1) games with other league clubs. But since A playing B is the same as B playing A, the total number of league games was ½x (x - 1).

Since 75 games in all were played, the Devon club played

75 - ½x (x - 1)

If we choose as a trial too small a value for x, the number of clubs in the league, we will find that the Devon club must play more than x games with league members, which is impossible. If we choose as a trial too large a value for x we shall find ½x (x - 1) is greater than 75. Simple trial gives

No. of league clubs	No. of league games	Total number of games	No. of Devon club games
10	45	75	30
11	55	75	20
12	66	75	9
13	78	75	—

The first two trials give the impossible result of more Devon club games than there are league clubs to play against, and the last trial gives a total of league games in excess of 75. Hence, the third trial is the only possible solution and there are 12 league clubs. The Devon club played 9 games with league clubs and was unable to arrange a game with 3 league clubs.

84: What Shape Is It?

The object is a round cylinder with a groove cut in the middle of one side (see Figure 25). The depth of the groove is such that the distance between the start and the end of the cut is equal to its width. Viewed from above, the object looks like Figure 26.

FIGURE 25

FIGURE 26

85: The Ten Bags

Number the bags for identification from 1 to 10. Take one weight from number 1 bag, three weights from number 3 bag, and so on up to ten weights from number 10 bag.

If all the weights were 16 ounces each, the total of these weights would be

$1 + 2 + 3 + 4 + 5 + 6 + 7 + 8 + 9 + 10 = 55$ pounds

If the bag with the 17-ounce weights is number X, the total weight will be

55 pounds + X ounces.

Hence, if we subtract 55 pounds from the total obtained in the weighing described, the excess in ounces will be the number of the bag containing the 17-ounce weights.

86: Tom's Class

This type of problem is best solved by use of a diagram. If we draw three overlapping circles representing the three subjects and indicate by numbers inside the circles the children who like each subject, the problem can be quickly solved. (See Figure 27) We can place 3 in the area covered by all three circles to represent the three children who liked all three subjects.

Now 16 said they liked English and Languages, and these must all be included in the shaded area consisting of the overlapping of the English and Languages circles. The 3 already indicated in the top half like all three subjects so the balance of 13 must be placed in the bottom half. These are the children who like English and Languages but do not like Mathematics. Proceeding in this manner, using the information that 7 liked both Mathematics and Languages and 25 in total liked Languages we have the representation shown in Figure 28. Proceeding similarly with the other information, we can complete the whole diagram. (See Figure 29) Counting the total number of children in each area of the diagram, we find there are 47 children in Tom's class.

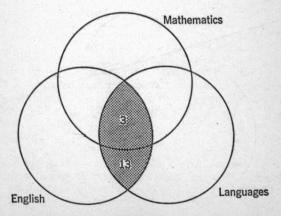

FIGURE 27

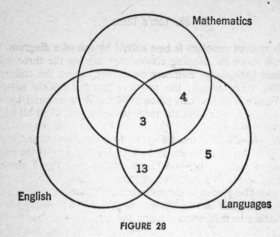

FIGURE 28

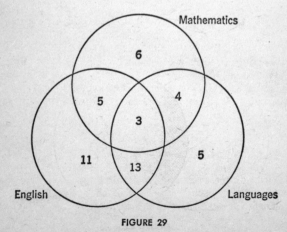

FIGURE 29

87: Mexican Table Mats

Let the number of circles along the top edge of the mat be x and the number of circles along the side of the mat be y. Then the total number of circles in the mat is

$$xy$$

and the number of circles around the edge is

$$2x + 2y - 4$$

Since this must be one-half the total number of circles we have

$$xy = 4x + 4y - 8$$
$$\therefore xy - 4x - 4y + 16 = 16 - 8$$
$$\text{and} \quad (x - 4)(y - 4) = 8$$

Since x and y must be integers, so must $(x - 4)$ and $(y - 4)$ and these must be factors of 8. The only integer factors of 8 are (8 and 1) or (4 and 2), which give x = 12 and y = 5, or x = 8 and y = 6. Hence, the mat must be

$$12 \text{ by } 5 \text{ circles}$$
$$\text{or} \quad 8 \text{ by } 6 \text{ circles}$$

88: Russian Roulette

Let us assume McGraw has x empty chambers and Hipshot y empty chambers.

The chance McGraw wins on his first shot is $(6 - x)/6$.

The chance McGraw and Hipshot both miss on their first shot is

$$x/6 \text{ multiplied by } y/6$$
$$= \frac{xy}{36}$$

We are told the chances of each winning the whole contest are equal, that is each has a one-half chance of winning the contest. Hence, McGraw's chance of winning the whole contest is ½ just before he shoots his first shot and, if they both miss on the first round, McGraw's chance will be ½ just before he shoots his second shot. Therefore,

$$½ = \begin{matrix}\text{Chance McGraw} \\ \text{wins on first shot}\end{matrix} + ½ \begin{matrix}\text{Chance both miss} \\ \text{on first shot}\end{matrix}$$

$$\text{or } ½ = \frac{6 - x}{6} + ½ \cdot \frac{xy}{36}$$

$$36 = 72 - 12x + xy$$

$$y = 12 - \frac{36}{x}$$

Now x, the number of empty chambers in McGraw's six-shooter, can equal only 1, 2, 3, 4, or 5, and the last is not possible because 36 is not divisible by 5. Trying each value in turn

x	$\frac{36}{x}$	$12 - \frac{36}{x}$	y
1	36	-24	
2	18	- 6	
3	12	0	0
4	9	3	3

Only the last solution is possible; hence, McGraw has 4 empty chambers and Hipshot 3. Therefore, McGraw has two bullets in his gun and Hipshot three bullets.

89: Hen Laying Problem

Laying an egg and a half in a day and a half is the same as laying an egg a day. Hence we are told that a hen and a half lays an egg a day. For the hens "who lay better by a half" we shall have a hen and a half lays an egg *and a half*, or these hens each lay an egg a day. A half-score and a half is $10 + ½ = 10½$ eggs and a week and a half is $7 + 3½ = 10½$

days. To lay 10½ eggs in 10½ days is the same as laying an egg a day. Hence, we require 1 hen, or "half a hen and a half."

The answer is, therefore, "half a hen."

90: The Curious Sequence

This is one of those nasty catchy puzzles. The real solution is

O T T F F S S E N . . .

being the initial letters of One, Two, Three, Four, Five, Six, etc.

91: Hex Sign

Let A and B be the end points of two neighboring petals and 0 the center of the hex sign (see Figure 30). Then AB = OA = OB = 1 inch.

We observe that one-half of one of the petals is equal to the difference between *the triangle ABO* and the segment of a circle (see Figure 31).

The triangle is an equilateral triangle with sides equal to one inch. The area of such a triangle can be calculated by the formula

½ Base x Height

Dropping a perpendicular line from one of the apexes to the middle of one of the sides, the height can be readily ascertained by the theory of Pythagoras to be

$$\sqrt{(1)^2 - (½)^2}$$

and since the base is 1 inch, the area is

½$\sqrt{1 - ¼}$ = ¼ $\sqrt{3}$ = 0.433 square inches

Turning to the segment of the circle in the right-hand illus-

tration, the angle at A is 60°, which is one sixth of 360°.
Therefore, the area of the segment is one sixth of the area
of a circle with 1 inch radius or

$$\frac{\pi}{6} = 0.524 \text{ square inches}$$

The difference between these two areas is the area of half a
petal.

Therefore, half a petal = 0.524 − 0.433
$$= 0.091 \text{ square inches}$$
and the area of a whole petal is
$$0.18 \text{ square inches}$$

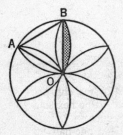

FIGURE 30

FIGURE 31

92: Large Numbers

The largest number formed from four ones is
$$11^{11^{11}} = 285{,}311{,}670{,}611$$
and the largest number formed from four twos is
$$22^{2^{2}}$$
which would involve over one and a quarter million digits if written out in full.

93: Professor Cubit's Bets

(1) At lunchtime the elevator is always in use and it goes up and down, stopping at various floors as requested. Professor Cubit's office, overlooking the campus, is high in the building and it is not very likely that the elevator is above him since it does not take long to travel from his floor to the top of the building and down again. It is much more likely that the elevator is below him, either on its way down to the ground floor or making the long climb up.

If the elevator is below the Professor when he presses both buttons, as is more likely, the up car will arrive first.

(2) The chance of the second digit being different from the first is 9/10 and the chance that the third digit will also be different again is 8/10, and so on for the whole eight digits. Hence, the chance of all eight digits being different is
$$\frac{9 \cdot 8 \cdot 7 \cdot 6 \cdot 5 \cdot 4 \cdot 3}{10 \cdot 10 \cdot 10 \cdot 10 \cdot 10 \cdot 10 \cdot 10} = \frac{181{,}440}{10{,}000{,}000}$$
Hence, my chances of winning the dollar are less than 2 in 100 and to pay a nickel for a chance worth less than 2 cents will be unprofitable in the long run.

94: The Bird Cage

If the bird is in a completely airtight box, the weight of the box and the bird will be the same whether the bird is flying or perching. If the bird is flying, its weight is borne by the air pressure on its wings; but this pressure is then transmitted by the air to the floor of the box. If the bird is flying in an open cage, part of the increase in pressure on the air is transmitted to the floor of the cage, but part is transmitted to the atmosphere outside the cage. Hence, the cage with the bird will be lighter if the bird is flying.

95: Diophantine Equations

The solution of this problem is much simplified by writing
$$x^2 + y^2 = z^2 + t^2$$
in the form
$$x^2 - t^2 = z^2 - y^2$$
whence
$$(x + t)(x - t) = (z + y)(z - y)$$

Simple trial soon shows the simplest solution is obtained by equating these two expressions to 15 whence

$$x + t = 15 \qquad\qquad x - t = 1$$
$$z + y = 5 \qquad\qquad z - y = 3$$

This gives $x = 8$, $t = 7$, $z = 4$, $y = 1$ or,
$$8^2 + 1^2 = 7^2 + 4^2 = 65$$

96: Crossing the Estuary

I must row up into the tide toward A instead of straight to my dock D, as indicated in the plan in Figure 32, if I am to make a landing at my dock. If it takes me a quarter as long again to cross the estuary, my actual speed of travel from T to D is $5/(1 + 1/4) = 4$ miles an hour.

Therefore, TA to TD is as 5 is to 4 and AD is proportional to

$$\sqrt{5^2 - 4^2} = 3$$

Hence, the tide is flowing at 3 miles an hour.

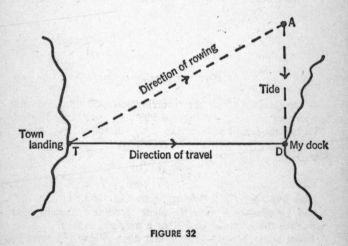

FIGURE 32

97: Colored Labels

C argues as follows:
(1) If A sees two blue labels he will know that his label is
    red and will declare this and since a little time has passed
    without this happening B and C cannot both have blue
    labels.
(2) Similarly, if B sees two blue labels he will know that his
    label is red and will declare this, and, hence, A and C
    cannot both have blue labels.
(3) C can now deduce that *if his label is blue,* both A and B
    must have red labels. Now C knows that both A and B are
    intelligent. If B had seen a red label on A's hat and a
    blue label on C's hat, he would know his hat did not have
    a blue label, because in this case A would have declared
    his label to be red.
(4) Since a little time has passed and neither A nor B has
    declared he could deduce the color of his label, C knows
    his label cannot be blue, and therefore must be red.

98: Find the Missing Digits

Since we have a four-step recurring decimal in the dividend,
the divisor must be a factor of 9999 or a multiple thereof.
This follows from the fact that
$$.1000100010001 \text{ etc.}$$
equals
$$\frac{1000}{9999}$$

Now 9999 has the following prime factors: 3, 11 and 101.
3 and 11 develop a more frequent recurrence than 4, and
hence the divisor must be 101 or a multiple thereof.

From lines (3) and (4) the first digit of line (4) must be
9. Hence, the divisor must be 101, 303 or 909. 101 is impossible because line (2) contains 4 digits. The first digit of

line (3) is 1 and hence line (2) must be 9292, 8282 or X3X3. The first two of these are not divisible by 303 or 909 and we find the only possible solution is 6363 and the divisor is 909.

The full solution is:

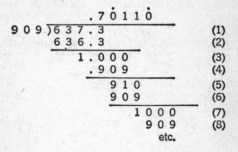

.70110	
909.)637.3	(1)
636.3	(2)
1.000	(3)
.909	(4)
910	(5)
909	(6)
1000	(7)
909	(8)
etc.	

99: A Curious Walk

The simple solution is that he started at the North Pole. Possibly he was one of the crew of the Seadragon, the submarine which broke through the ice at the Pole a few years ago. His three-mile walk clearly brings him back to base (see Figure 33).

The more difficult solution is in the neighborhood of the South Pole (see Figure 34). Starting from A he walks 1 mile south to B; he then walks eastward around the Pole to B again and from B north to A. The distance of A from the South Pole will be very nearly $1 + \dfrac{1}{2\pi}$ miles if his one mile turn of the Pole is once around. If twice around, it will be $1 + \dfrac{1}{4\pi}$. If three times around, $1 + \dfrac{1}{6\pi}$, and so on for more turns around the Pole.

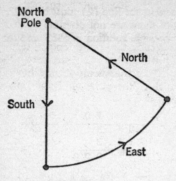

FIGURE 33

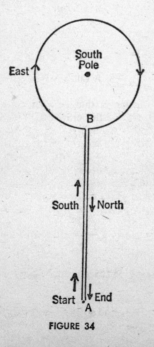

FIGURE 34

100: Football Logic

There are only three possibilities for the true facts.
(i) All the friends are on the football team.
(ii) Some, but not all, the friends are on the football team.
(iii) None of the friends are on the football team.
If against each of these we put T for True and F for False
for each statement:

	Facts	(1)	(2)	(3)
(i)	All	T	F	F
(ii)	Some but not all	F	T	T
(iii)	None	F	T	F

Looking at this chart we see (2) and (3) would be true if
some, but not all, the friends were on the football team and
they would be false if all the friends were on the football team.
Similarly (1) and (3) can both be false but cannot both be
true and (1) and (2) cannot both be true and cannot both
be false.